THE OFFICIAL **PET GUIDE**

Care for Your

Gerbil

CONTENTS

HarperCollins*Publishers*

First published in 1980 by
William Collins Sons & Co Ltd
Revised edition 1985

New edition published in 1994
by HarperCollins Publishers
London

Reprinted 1995, 1996, 1997, 1998

This is a fully revised and extended edition of *Care for your Gerbil*, first
published in 1980 and reprinted 4 times, with revisions in 1985

© Royal Society for the Prevention of Cruelty to Animals 1980, 1994

Text of the 1980 edition by Tina Hearne; text revisions and additions
for this edition by Michael Pollard
Designed and edited by The Templar Company plc
Pippbrook Mill, London Road, Dorking, Surrey RH4 1JE

Front cover photograph: Animal Ark, London
Text photographs: Trevor J. Hill

Illustrations by Colin Newman (Bernard Thornton Artists)

**A catalogue record for this book is available
from the British Library**

ISBN 0 00 412731 5

Printed in Hong Kong by Sing Cheong Printing Co. Ltd.

First things first, animals are fun. Anybody who has ever enjoyed the company of a pet knows well enough just how strong the bond between human and animal can be. Elderly or lonely people often depend on a pet for their only company, and this can be a rewarding relationship for both human and animal. Doctors have proved that animals can be instrumental in the prevention of and recovery from mental or physical disease. Children learn the meaning of loyalty, unselfishness and friendship by growing up with animals.

But the commitment to an animal doesn't begin and end with a visit to the local pet shop. A pet should never be given as a 'surprise' present. The decision to bring a pet into your home should always be discussed and agreed by all the members of your family. Bear in mind that parents are ultimately responsible for the health and well-being of the animal for the whole of its lifetime. If you are not prepared for the inevitable expense, time, patience and occasional frustration involved, then the RSPCA would much rather that you didn't have a pet.

Armed with the facts, aware of the pitfalls but still confident of your ability to give a pet a good home, the next step is to find where you can get an animal from. Seek the advice of a veterinary surgeon or RSPCA Inspector about reputable local breeders or suppliers. Do consider the possibility of offering a home to an animal from an RSPCA establishment. There are no animals more deserving of loving owners.

As for the care of your pet, you should find in this book all you need to know to keep it happy, healthy and rewarding for many years to come. Responsible ownership means happy pets. Enjoy the experience!

Terence C. Bate

TERENCE BATE BVSc, LLB, MRCVS
Chief Veterinary Officer, RSPCA

Introduction

Mongolian gerbils have been kept as pets in Britain only since 1964. The first breeding pairs arrived in that year, intended as laboratory animals, but their qualities as delightful pets soon became obvious. They rapidly became established as one of the most successful pets ever introduced into this country, especially for families living in homes which are not suitable for larger animals.

GERBILS ARE:
- Diurnal. This means that they are awake and active during the day, when they can be observed and enjoyed.
- Hardy. In the wild they have to survive in very difficult conditions, and they carry this characteristic into captivity.
- Clean. Their natural habitat is the desert, where they need to conserve liquid. Consequently, they pass very little urine. There is no smell from healthy gerbils.
- Quiet and docile with people.
- Inquisitive, agile and active. They enjoy playing with simple toys and investigating new ones.
- Tame when handled. Any aggressiveness is almost always due to mishandling.
- Agreeably sociable when housed in compatible groups.

The golden agouti is closest in colouring to the wild Mongolian gerbil, but the black and albino are among the several colour variations now available.

As gerbils live in colonies in their natural habitat, it is not advisable to keep one gerbil on its own. If you do not want to breed from your gerbils, two females from the same litter will live together in harmony for life and be a constant source of interest for the whole family. For breeding, a monogamous pair introduced at the age of puberty should be housed together for life, even when breeding. The male will take an active part in tunnelling and shredding nesting materials and poses no threat to the suckling young.

Gerbils are best housed in a gerbilarium in which they may dig and burrow as in the wild. It is possible, though risky, to keep several generations of gerbils together as in the wild in an extended family group. The risk is that, in practice, there will not be enough space for the gerbils to establish their own territories and fighting will break out among them.

Mongolian gerbils are compact animals with neat movements that mirror their way of life. Their instinct is to keep themselves and their surroundings clean and tidy.

Although naturally timid, gerbils adapt well to domestication provided they are approached and handled with care, and given time to adjust to new surroundings.

Choosing a gerbil

WHERE TO BUY GERBILS

Gerbils are easily obtained from pet shops, but there are two other sources that should be considered. If you are interested in breeding or showing gerbils, the best place to buy them is from a recognized breeder who exhibits regularly at shows. The local RSPCA inspector, library or vet should be able to put you in touch with reputable breeders, clubs and show organizers in your area.

Alternatively, you could consider buying from a friend or acquaintance who breeds and has surplus youngsters. In this case, however, carry out the health checks detailed on page 35 before you buy.

HOW MANY AND WHICH SEX?

A pair is the minimum number of gerbils you should buy. They may be one male and one female – for breeding – or, if you do not want to breed, two females from the same litter. Two males, or females from different litters, will fight.

In the wild, gerbils live in colonies of equal numbers of males and females. It is possible, but difficult, to reproduce this

The golden agouti is sandy-haired with a black stripe and white underside

pattern of living in captivity. Each pair needs enough room to establish its own adequate territory, and an extensive gerbilarium would be needed, which may be impractical in a small home.

WHEN TO BUY
The best time to buy gerbils is when they are between six and eight weeks old, and certainly before ten weeks. It is virtually impossible to pair up adult gerbils, even for breeding as they will fight any gerbil they do not consider part of their extended family.

It is important to plan for your gerbils' arrival in advance so that you have time to arrange for housing. Do not be tempted into a spur-of-the-moment purchase without adequate preparation.

It is best to avoid buying gerbils round about Christmas time: there is far too much noise and excitement in the home at Christmas for your gerbils to settle in peacefully and get the right amount (but not too much) attention. If you want to give a child gerbils as a Christmas present, it's far better to make a present of a gerbilarium or cage (see pages 16–21) together with a *promise* that the animals will be chosen when the holiday period is over.

WHAT TO LOOK FOR
It's all too tempting to make a rush choice, especially when young children are involved. Take your time, and see as many young gerbils as you can before making a final decision. Study the health checks on page 35 and keep them in mind.

Healthy gerbils are timid but also naturally inquisitive. If you move and speak quietly, they will come forward after a while and take a nut or a piece of grain from your fingers. Avoid any that seem lethargic or shrink away to a corner of the cage.

Gerbils offered for sale in Britain are normally bred here. But gerbils from abroad are, like all other mammals, subject to quarantine regulations designed to prevent rabies from entering Britain. These stipulate a six-month period of isolation on entry.

GETTING READY

Before you buy your gerbils, you should already be prepared for their arrival in your home. They will need a cage or gerbilarium (see pages 16–21), with a supply of suitable bedding. The siting of this is of critical importance. It must be away from draughts and direct sunlight, and in a room where the temperature stays above 20°C/70°F for much of the day. Gerbils should be housed in a room not accessible to cats or dogs.

You will also need a supply of food (see pages 28–31) and a toy or two (see pages 20–21). Remember that it is important to introduce gerbils into your home at a time when life is calm and quiet.

Newly arrived gerbils should be allowed to investigate their surroundings at their own pace. A maze of tunnels to explore will soon make them feel at home.

Two-tier cages provide greater opportunities for climbing and play than an ordinary cage.

Varieties

The basic colouring of the Mongolian gerbil is sandy, with pale hair on the underside and a line of dark guard hairs down the length of the spine and tail, which is tipped with black. The claws are also black.

The L-shaped stance often adopted by gerbils, with fore-legs raised off the ground and tail stretched out behind, is characteristic of the species. The long hind legs enable gerbils to cover large areas of ground in search of scarce food in their natural desert habitat.

As gerbils have been domesticated for only thirty years, there has not yet been time for the development of a large number of colour varieties. Varieties are bred from individual young with attractive colour mutations. Selective breeding has to be done with care to avoid the risk of deformity so the number of colour varieties so far available is small.

The Golden Agouti is the most common variety of gerbil, with the sandy hair and dark stripe already described. If you buy from a pet shop, this is the variety you are most likely to find on sale.

The Albino was one of the first variations to appear. Its skin, fur and whiskers are white and its eyes are pink. This coloration is the result of the absence of pigment in the body, a condition known as albinism.

The full range of colour variations currently available in Britain. If you want to keep some of the less common variations, you may have to go to a specialist breeder.

White Spot

Black

Dark-tailed White

Albino

The Dark-tailed White is indistinguishable from the albino until the age of about three months. It then develops a dark line along the length of its tail.

The Black was first bred in the USA and has since been imported into Britain. It has an abnormal level of black pigment in the body. This condition, known as melanism, is the opposite of albinism.

The Cinnamon is another breed developed in the early days. Its pale, short coat is due to the absence of the Golden Agouti's long, dark guard hairs.

The White Spot and the **Canadian White Spot** are similar in overall colouring to the Golden Agouti, but they have patches of white on the head, paws and the tip of the tail. The White Spot has one patch of white on the forehead. The Canadian White Spot has another on the back of its neck.

The Dove has an overall dove-grey coat.

The Argenté has the sandy Golden Agouti coat, but with a silvery sheen.

Dove

Argenté

Canadian White Spot

Cinnamon

Biology

On 14 April 1866, the French naturalist, the Abbé David, who was journeying through Mongolia and China, wrote in his diary that 'This morning I acquired three yellow rats I do not yet know the name of, having long, hairy tails.' He sent specimens to Paris, but the zoologists there were similarly unable to identify them. These were Mongolian gerbils, and they had never before been seen in Europe.

At the Museum of Natural History in Paris they were given the scientific name *Meriones unguiculatus*. *Unguiculatus* (Latin, *unguis*, a nail) is a name that can be applied to any mammal with claws. Meriones was a Greek warrior with tusks on his helmet. It suggests, perhaps, that the specimens were being kept together, and not surprisingly to us, with the benefit of hindsight, were fighting among themselves, with tooth and nail.

Rodents The gerbils belong to the order of rodents, the most numerous and widespread of all the mammals. The rodents are distinguished by their highly specialized teeth (see Teeth), adapted for gnawing. The word rodent is derived from the Latin, *rodere*, to gnaw.

The rodents, which so often fall victim to birds of prey and to the carnivorous mammals, may seem lowly, but their very insignificance, together with a natural caution and high fertility helps to account for their biological success. Another factor, significant in the case of the gerbil, is that they have colonized and adapted to some very harsh environments that less versatile mammals need to avoid.

Tail The Mongolian gerbil has a distinctive long, furry tail with a black tip. Adult gerbils are often seen to have lost the tip, for it can be shed during a fight. In nature it is a biological safety device, a means by which a fleet gerbil can escape, although once only, for it never grows again, from a predator that seizes it only by the tip.

Some other species, but it is thought not the Mongolian gerbil, use the tail to store fat for the winter months. It is, however, a useful balance in running and jumping, and in sitting upright in this very characteristic position.

Balancing on the tail

Fur Since deserts and heat are so closely associated in our minds, it sometimes surprises people that desert rodents, such as gerbils, should be furry. The reason is that, instead of experiencing perpetual heat, the desert rodents have to contend with great variations of temperature.

In the desert, a day of searing heat can be followed by a frosty night. Similarly, in the Mongolian desert, the hot summer months are followed by a long, cold winter with snow that traps the gerbils underground for weeks at a time.

The Mongolian gerbil has fur even on the pads of its feet. This fur not only gives protection against uncomfortable surface temperatures, but also prevents the gerbil from sinking into sandy soil, and so losing speed, when it needs to run fast to escape from predators.

Teeth Gerbils have the same dental formula as rats and mice: 2 incisors and 6 molars in either jaw, making a total of 16. There are no canines, and no pre-molars, which means there is a large gap, the diastema, between the front and the back teeth. Rodents are able to keep splinters and the like out of their mouths when gnawing by drawing the cheeks into the diastema to form a barrier.

Gerbils, like all rodents, must gnaw. Only in this way are they able to reduce the length of the incisors, which grow continuously. Overgrown incisors can cause death, either by preventing feeding, or, if one is lost, by its opposite number growing, unopposed, until it pierces the brain or locks into the other jaw.

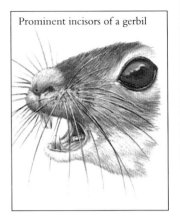
Prominent incisors of a gerbil

Black claws of Mongolian gerbil

Claws Before the Rabies (Importation of Mammals) Order, 1971 came into effect in Britain, several different species of gerbil and related animals were being taken directly from the wild and imported into Britain from Asia and Africa, regardless of disease risk. It was soon found, however, that of all these, only the Mongolian gerbil was a suitable animal for domestication. They were bred in Britain, and by the time the 1971 Order came into

force there was no need to import more from the wild.

The feature that distinguishes the Mongolian gerbil from other species is the black claws, five to each limb. In the wild the claws are a tool for digging; in captivity they may become overgrown from lack of use. They are composed of keratin, a lightweight, horny substance that can be cut by a vet, for they grow from a sensitive core that supplies them with nerves and blood vessels.

Gerbils in the desert

The Mongolian gerbil in the wild lives in harsh desert and semi–desert conditions, where rainfall is low, vegetation is sparse and temperatures fluctuate wildly between summer and winter and between night and day.

The main reason the gerbils survive is that they are able to burrow into the deep, sandy soils for protection from extremes of temperature. Although the summers are very hot and the winters very cold, at a depth of 0.5m/18in underground the summer temperature is constant and tolerable and the gerbils are also safe from the sub-zero winter temperatures.

The burrows are a complex, linked system of horizontal galleries, each on a different level. At the centre of each level is a round nest lined with grasses and flanked by food storage chambers. Here the gerbils are able to hoard food for the long winter when they may be trapped underground by deep snow on the surface.

Near human habitation, on the fringes of their area, the gerbils are able to feed off steppe-land grasses and crops of wheat and millet; those living deeper in the desert will have to search more diligently for wind-blown seeds, green plants that burst into growth after rain and perhaps insects.

The burrowing habit is important, not only because it allows the gerbils to enjoy more moderate temperatures, but also because it prevents their becoming dehydrated in the dry desert air. In their holes deep underground the humidity will be much higher than on the surface, and consequently the gerbils will lose little water through respiration.

Gerbils also conserve their body fluids by not sweating and by re-absorbing their liquid intake, which other animals would excrete, producing instead highly concentrated urine and dry faeces.

In very severe conditions, the gerbils as a species can even survive for a while underground without water, although individuals may perish.

Artist's impression of gerbils' natural habitat in Mongolia. Each gallery, complete with its own nest and food storage chambers, is occupied by a separate breeding pair.

The gerbilarium

By far the most satisfactory way of housing gerbils is in a gerbilarium. Here, they can burrow and live a social life, although on a much smaller scale than in the wild. A large glass tank with a thick layer of a suitable burrowing medium provides gerbils with the comfort, security and privacy of a small underground retreat. It also allows room for a greater variety of movement and activity. From the owner's point of view, a gerbilarium has the advantages that the gerbils can be observed easily and maintained with very little effort, with the reward of seeing them behave as naturally as possible in close captivity.

The basis of a gerbilarium is a large aquarium tank, which may be bought second-hand. (The glass or plastic should be sound, but it does not have to be waterproof as no water is to be put in it.) The minimum size is about 75cm/30in long, 40cm/16in wide and 30cm/12in tall. The aquarium should be thoroughly cleaned before it is adapted for its new role.

Unless the aquarium has its own ventilation cover, it is essential to provide a tightly fitting lid to prevent escapes. This can be made of small-gauge wire mesh firmly stapled to a wooden frame. The wood of the frame should not be accessible to the gerbils, as they can gnaw through it.

The siting of the gerbilarium is important. It will in itself be draught-proof, but it should be placed away from radiators and where no direct sunlight will fall on it. Overheating of the tank will cause possible dehydration and heat exhaustion.

The gerbils will need a thick layer of material in which to burrow and nest. The best burrowing medium is a mixture of Irish moss peat and chopped straw. Some pre-packed seed compost could also be added. You will need enough to form a layer about 15cm/6in deep on the floor of the gerbilarium. Use a bucket to mix it thoroughly before putting it in place. Breeding gerbils kept in a gerbilarium will not need a nesting-box as they will make their own nest underground.

Clean white paper is the best choice for bedding. Do not use newspaper or other paper which has been printed, as the ink may be poisonous.

Burrowing medium The burrowing medium should be compacted down so that the gerbils' tunnels will hold their shape without collapsing. Once dug, the burrows do not necessarily remain constant. Frequently gerbils will re-excavate the tank, or part of it, particularly if they have been disturbed.

Bedding Clean paper for bedding may be torn into manageable pieces and lightly crumpled. The gerbils will drag it underground and shred it to make their own nests.

Playthings Simple objects such as cardboard tubes or wooden cotton reels will provide the gerbils with the toys they enjoy.

Gerbilarium cover A secure cover for the gerbilarium is essential. Gerbils are extremely agile and they could easily jump out.

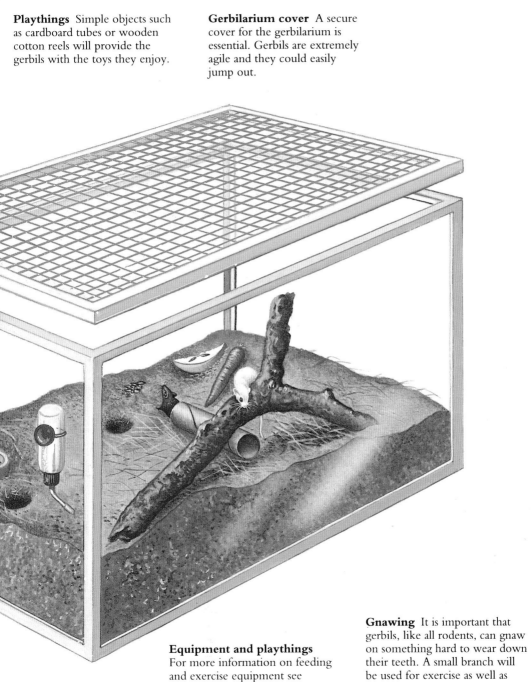

Equipment and playthings
For more information on feeding and exercise equipment see pages 20–23.

Gnawing It is important that gerbils, like all rodents, can gnaw on something hard to wear down their teeth. A small branch will be used for exercise as well as gnawing.

Cages

It is difficult to be satisfied with the caging of gerbils after seeing them in a gerbilarium, but two types of cage can be considered. If there is any merit in caging, it is that the gerbils may be more easily accessible and this might sometimes be an advantage.

The minimum size of cage for two gerbils is about 60cm/24in long, 25cm/10in wide and at least 25cm/10in high. To withstand the gerbils' constant gnawing it must be made of metal, so home-made cages are not a practical possibility. Commercially made cages are of metal mesh with a metal tray as a base. Before you buy, check that the cage will fit on to a stable base in your home out of the way of draughts and direct sunlight.

Ramps and galleries are desirable, not only because they considerably extend the floor area, but because they are a substitute for the gallery systems the gerbils would excavate in the wild.

It is imperative that the gerbils be given a nesting box and nesting materials for their rest periods during the day, and for sleeping. Some privacy and darkness are very important to burrowing animals which in nature spend so much time underground.

This cage is about 60cm/2 ft long. By ingenious use of ramps and galleries it allows the gerbils maximum freedom to move around in the cage, but a cage of larger dimensions would be preferable. The nesting box is essential to provide darkness, warmth and seclusion for sleep, and a refuge if the gerbils are frightened.

The floor of the cage needs to have an ample covering of litter which the gerbils can tunnel through and use to pile up in the corners for extra cover. The litter may be looser material than in a gerbilarium as, although the gerbils will play with it, they have a nesting box to sleep in and will not need to establish permanent burrows. Suitable materials for caged gerbils include sawdust, wood chippings or peat, but do ensure that the sawdust or chippings are from wood that has not been chemically treated or painted.

Glass sheets, as used in budgerigar cages to prevent spillage, will stop the litter being flung out when the gerbils burrow into it.

Once they have acclimatized themselves, gerbils will soon start to arrange the litter to their own liking. There may be some spillage of material outside the cage unless low glass sides are fitted.

MULTI-STOREY BOX CAGE

The multi-storey box cage is another that is suitable for accommodating gerbils and may be better than the box cage. The various ladders and storeys allow the gerbils scope for movement within the confines of a cage; the nest box provides privacy and darkness and a 'basement' tank can be furnished as a small gerbilarium for burrowing. This type of cage is sometimes sold for keeping mice, but providing the size is generous enough, it provides a satisfactory home for a pair of gerbils.

Equipping the cage or gerbilarium

NESTING BOX

A nesting box is required only for caged gerbils. Various designs are available from pet shops. The box should be sited in a corner of the cage in a position which gives maximum security and darkness at night. Your gerbils may have a distinct preference for one site over another, so if they seem reluctant to use the nesting box experiment with different positions within the cage. Once a site has been found to their liking, stick to it, returning the box to the same position after cleaning the cage, for example.

The gerbils will shred pieces of clean white paper or unbleached kitchen roll for bedding and may pile up litter round the entrance to suit their needs. As well as using the nesting box for sleep and rest, they will use it as a bolthole if they feel threatened or uneasy. In these circumstances, they should not be disturbed.

FEEDING AND DRINKING

The gerbils' food bowl should be made of stout pottery with straight sides, and heavy enough not to be knocked over easily. A bowl about 12cm/5in in diameter will enable two gerbils to feed easily at the same time.

Water must be available at all times from a gravity-fed bottle attached to the side of the cage or gerbilarium, or suspended securely from the top.

GNAWING BLOCK

Gerbils need to trim their teeth by gnawing, or the teeth grow too long. Commercial gnawing blocks are available at pet shops, but a block of wood, with any splinters sanded off, is just as good provided it has not been treated or painted.

ENVIRONMENT

Gerbils live active daytime lives and need a stimulating environment. Permanent features of the gerbilarium or cage might include one or two large flints or pebbles which they

Nesting box

Drinking bottle

Food bowl

Gnawing block

Ladder

Playthings from household items

can climb over, and a dead branch which will be used for both climbing and gnawing. If there is room, wooden ramps and ladders may be added.

A wide variety of assorted objects may be added to stimulate the gerbils' interest. 'Gerbil toys' are available from pet shops, but everyday objects will serve just as well. These include a cardboard tube from a roll of kitchen towel or toilet paper, wooden cotton-reels, a small clay flower-pot, an old mug, a jam-jar, a fibre (not plastic) egg-box cut in half, and a child's old shoe or sandal with any metal parts removed. Metal, plastic and painted wooden toys should be avoided. So should any objects made of fabric or foam material which could be chewed and eaten.

Gerbils should not be confused or over-excited by being given too many playthings at once. Two or three items in the gerbilarium or cage will suffice at any one time, and can be changed for others every few days. You will soon discover which playthings excite the most interest and enjoyment.

Common household objects provide just as much fun for gerbils as special toys bought in a pet shop. Playthings should be kept clean, and removed when they start to show signs of wear.

Exercise

Wheels can be useful devices for play and exercise, but need to be used with caution. This solid type, with no spokes to trap feet or tail, is thought safe.

Gerbils are highly active, agile animals, able to bound and jink, to jump and climb and burrow. Those which in the wild live in true desert conditions, with scant food available, have to travel long distances and sift the soil laboriously in order to find sustenance. In captivity they need scope for plenty of movement, and caged gerbils, in particular, benefit from being taken out of their cage for a while each day.

EXERCISE: GERBILARIUM
In captivity, gerbils will exercise and be most naturally occupied if they are housed in a big gerbilarium, where they can develop a system of tunnels that allows them to approximate, to some extent, the wild life-style.

EXERCISE: CAGE
Gerbils can be reasonably well exercised in a cage providing it is fitted with ramps, ladders and more than one storey. They need to be able to move around the cage as they would around the gallery complexes they excavate in the wild. In a cage it is also an advantage to put down a really deep floor litter for the gerbils to career through and lengths of piping for them to use as substitute burrows and bolt holes.

EXERCISE: WHEEL
The use of exercise wheels is a cause of some argument among gerbil experts. There is no doubt that gerbils greatly enjoy using these wheels, so much so that it can become compulsive. But there is a slight risk of animals getting a tail or leg caught, or of exhausting themselves.

   If an exercise wheel is used, it should have a solid wheel and back, without spokes. With this type, if the gerbil should slip it will simply fall harmlessly out. Some types can be screwed to a firm base, but it may be advisable to restrict the gerbils' access to the wheel if they go on exercising with it, denying themselves rest until they are exhausted. In this case, the wheel is best placed in the gerbilarium or cage for a few hours a day, but ensure they have other amusements.

EXERCISE: INDOORS

If conditions permit, gerbils may be allowed out of their gerbilarium or cage to exercise in the room under supervision. Any other animals should, of course, be excluded and the doors and windows must be closed. Watch out also for open chimneys or cupboards, small breakable ornaments and any other hazards.

Gerbils may hide themselves away and be reluctant to return to the gerbilarium or cage, especially when young. They will eventually return for food, but may be tempted back beforehand with a titbit.

EXERCISE: OUTDOORS

Provision for the gerbils to exercise outdoors in good weather may be made by the use of a small-mesh run, which must be built with a solid base. Gerbils may experience sore hocks if they are kept on wire mesh.

Gerbils value human company, and will treat their owner's hand as just another plaything to be investigated and enjoyed. Daily playtime out of the cage helps to keep gerbils alert and active, and to bond them to their owner.

Hygiene and grooming

ACCOMMODATION

No caged animal is easier to keep clean than the gerbil. Physical adaptation to its native deserts ensures that the gerbils waste little body fluid, excreting only dry faeces and concentrated urine. In the highly absorbent peat of a gerbilarium, in particular, the animals may remain living in sanitary conditions for three or four months before they need to be cleaned out and provided with fresh burrowing mixture. In school a gerbilarium may last a full term before refurbishing.

A certain amount of daily attention to the cage or gerbilarium is important and may determine how often it needs thorough cleaning. If perishable food is not left lying around to become stale or be buried, and if the gerbils are not allowed to pile up litter under the water bottle to make it leak, then the accommodation as a whole will need far less attention.

GROOMING

A pair of gerbils will keep themselves, each other and their young so clean that no attention is needed from the owner.

Dismantling and thoroughly cleaning the cage with soapy water is an infrequent chore with gerbils. They are such clean animals that this operation is probably not necessary more than three times a year.

Social grooming is one of the gerbils' many attractive habits – one they should not be deprived of by being kept singly.

Although gerbils need only a small amount of regular attention, this small amount is important. The daily schedule can fit easily into the routine of a household, for example when children come home from school.

Routine care for your gerbils

Daily	● Remove any wilting fruit and greenstuff, checking that none has been buried in the litter. ● Remove stale food and rinse the bowl before putting in a fresh supply. ● Empty, rinse and refill the water bottle. Check that the area under the spout is free of litter.
Weekly	● For caged gerbils, change the floor litter. There is no need to disturb the nesting box.
Every 3-4 months	● Dismantle the cage and clean it thoroughly with soapy water or disinfectant, rinsing afterwards with plain hot water. Renew all litter and bedding. You will need a suitable container to house the gerbils while this is going on. ● Remove, wash and rinse all toys. ● With a gerbilarium, remove the burrowing material and renew it, compacting it as before. Wash and rinse the sides and base.

Female cinnamon gerbil

Black gerbil

Typical Mongolian gerbils

Albino gerbil

Feeding

Mongolian gerbils in the wild feed mainly on seeds, grains, roots, stems and leaves. This diet is imitated in the ready-mixed packets of gerbil food available at pet shops. A typical mixture contains canary and sunflower seed, wheat, maize, millet, oats and barley. About 15g/½oz (about one table-spoonful) should be provided daily for each adult gerbil.

Gerbils should be given one meal a day. Gerbils in captivity, unlike those in the wild, do not hoard food, even in winter. This is thought to be because in temperate climates temperatures are not low enough to trigger the hoarding instinct. Unwanted food will be left, although some may be buried accidentally. Any surplus food should be cleared away daily and fresh food provided, making any necessary adjustments according to the amount consumed.

The mixed seed diet needs to be supplemented by fresh fruit and vegetables such as banana, apple, Brussels sprouts and cabbage, with hay and possibly extra protein in the form of hard-boiled egg, milk powder, grated cheese, and

Feed a basic diet of grains, seeds, hay and fresh vegetables. Favoured titbits include raisins, sunflower seeds and melon seeds.

Although healthy gerbils are keen on their food, they do not eat more than they need, and they do not take food away to hoard it. But do not save food from day to day. Throw away any leftovers and provide a fresh supply daily.

cat or dog food. These should be given in very small amounts. Your gerbils will also enjoy occasional titbits such as raisins, sunflower seeds, melon seeds and unsalted peanuts.

Wild plants such as wild grasses, groundsel, dandelion, chickweed, clover and nettle may be fed, but they should not be gathered from the roadside where they will have been polluted by traffic fumes. In any case, rinse all fruit, vegetables and wild plants under the tap before feeding them. Gerbils are very susceptible to poisoning by the small residues of insecticide spray that may be present on unwashed fruit and vegetable food.

When gerbils feed, they sit up erect on their hind legs and pick up the food with their front paws. If you observe your gerbils at feeding time, you will find out which foods are most appreciated and which are less popular.

WATER IN THE DIET
Gerbils must have fresh drinking water available at all times. The inverted gravity-fed bottle is the only satisfactory way of providing this. Gerbils take on average about a teaspoonful of water a day, but this amount can vary with the proportion of liquid taken in with fruit and vegetable food. Pregnant, nursing, sick and old gerbils may need up to two teaspoonfuls of water daily. The important point is that although gerbils drink very little and use water so economically, in captivity a small daily intake is vital to them regardless of diet. Care must be taken to ensure that the water is changed daily and the bottle filled. Sometimes gerbils will accidentally empty it by building up litter beneath the spout; check for this at least once daily.

PREGNANT AND NURSING GERBILS
Added protein such as cheese and hard-boiled egg should be provided in the diet of pregnant and nursing gerbils. Vitamin supplements, available from vets and pet shops, may also be given, but ensure that these are specifically formulated for gerbils.

Again, remember that pregnant and nursing gerbils may double their water intake, so check frequently that the water bottle is full.

FEEDING YOUNG GERBILS
Young gerbils can begin to eat solid food when they are three weeks old and should be fully weaned at four weeks. Sometimes the mother will help in the weaning process by

You will soon discover which treats your gerbils like best. Try tiny amounts of cheese, hard-boiled eggs and pet food. Wash all fruit and vegetables well.

pushing the young away from her if they approach her for milk, forcing them to take solid food.

Young gerbils' first solid food should consist of small seeds, canary rearing seed and a little washed fruit or vegetable. The more demanding protein foods mentioned above, such as hard-boiled egg and cheese, should not be fed until the young are about six weeks old.

Young gerbils should be eating the same food as their parents by about four weeks, but they should not be given titbits such as cheese until they are about six weeks old.

Handling

Gerbils are docile and even-tempered. Only rarely do they bite or scratch, and this is usually because they have been made nervous by careless handling.

Gerbils soon become tame with handling, but great care has to be taken. They are easily stressed by frequent or harsh handling, and since their movements are so quick they are liable to leap from the hand suddenly.

A gerbil should always be picked up from the front. This avoids surprising it, and also means that if it should suddenly leap it will cling to your clothing. Gerbils should be handled over a table or cushion to prevent a serious fall.

The usual way to hold a gerbil is in the cupped hands, lightly but firmly enough to prevent it from escaping. Alternatively, gerbils may be encouraged to walk on to one outstretched hand and be restrained with the other hand over the back.

Experienced handlers have the habit of trapping the base of the tail between the fingers for extra security, but the tail must always be handled gently. Careless handling can strip off the black tuft at the tip or even strip the whole outer skin.

Strong natural curiosity overcomes timidity. Most gerbils will explore a proffered hand.

Always remember that gerbils have a fragile bone structure and must be handled with a light, gentle touch. They will usually enjoy the warmth of the hand and the pleasure of being stroked too much to try to escape.

For this reason, gerbils must never be picked up by the tail.

Slow familiarization with young gerbils is the key to handling them with confidence on both sides. New pets should be allowed to sniff and explore the owner's fingers, be stroked on the head and ears, and spoken to quietly for several periods before any attempt is made to pick them up. If it is the gerbil which makes the first move by exploring the owner's outstretched hand, so much the better.

Pregnant gerbils must not be handled once they have retired to the nest or nesting box to give birth, and must not be disturbed during the birth itself. Both parents and young must be left undisturbed until the young begin to explore their surroundings at about seven days, and the young should not be handled until at least three weeks old unless this is urgently necessary for health reasons.

A gerbil must **NEVER** be picked up by the tail. In the wild, a gerbil can shed its tail to escape an enemy, but the tail will not grow again. Less dramatically, careless handling may strip the black tail tuft or the tail skin.

The healthy gerbil

A healthy gerbil is busy and inquisitive, carrying into the captive environment its natural instinct to be always on the hunt for food. It will investigate anything new or unusual and during its waking hours will not show signs of lethargy. The eyes should be bright and the nose, eyes and ears clean with no signs of discharge. They have the rodent's natural hardiness, but also a very small body size, which means they have only poor recuperative powers. If your gerbil falls ill, veterinary advice must be sought promptly, or the animal will rapidly deteriorate.

GNAWING

Gnawing is an essential feature of life for a healthy gerbil. The front incisor teeth grow continually throughout life and need to be worn down by gnawing. If they are allowed to become overgrown, they will gradually force apart the jaws and eventually make it impossible for the gerbil to feed.

This is the value of a tree branch in the cage or gerbilarium which will provide ample opportunity for gerbils to employ their gnawing instinct. Alternatives include the gnawing blocks available from pet shops, blocks of untreated wood, wooden toys, and large nuts such as brazils or walnuts.

Gerbils' propensity to gnaw should always be borne in mind when introducing other toys, and dictates against the use of plastic materials.

THE CAPTIVE ENVIRONMENT

In their natural habitat, Mongolian gerbils have to cope with very harsh conditions. In the desert, temperatures soar by day and drop, often to below freezing-point, at night. As diurnal animals, gerbils spend the cold nights asleep in their deep burrows. It is a common misunderstanding to equate desert animals with heat tolerance. Gerbils survive the extreme heat of the desert only by spending the hottest part of the day deep underground and confining all their activity to dawn and to late afternoon when the temperature is at its lowest daytime level.

Even in a gerbilarium with a deep layer of burrowing material, gerbils cannot reach the depths which insulate them from heat in the wild. At the same time, central heating and direct sunlight in the home can raise temperatures to unacceptable levels. Gerbils should never be housed where direct sunlight falls on their cage or gerbilarium, and they should be well away from radiators and other heat sources.

The optimum temperature range for the room in which gerbils are kept is 20°–24°C/68°–75°F. It is worth hanging a thermometer on the outside of the cage or gerbilarium to check that temperatures stay within this range.

If, despite these precautions, gerbils suffer from heat exhaustion, see page 36.

SIGNS OF HEALTH

Abdomen free from wounds; not distended; rubbed over objects to mark territory with sebaceous gland.

Anus clean; no staining or scouring.

Appetite good, eating approximately 1 tbs hard food daily, with fruit or vegetables and usually water.

Claws worn down naturally by constant digging and scratching.

Coat smooth and clean, with no bald patches or parasites.

Demeanour periods of great activity alternated with periods of rest. Alert, inquisitive and gentle.

Droppings small and dry.

Eyes clear, bright, without discharge; no inflammation or protrusion of third eyelid.

Feet no deformity; no soreness of hocks; used to drum an alert and a mating signal.

Movement agile, quick; often sits erect, balancing on hind legs.

Nose no soreness; no bald spots; no broken skin; no discharge.

Teeth incisors worn down naturally by constant gnawing. When the mouth is closed, the teeth should not be visible.

Tail whole, with the tip intact and no vertebrae exposed.

Urine small volumes only, not pink coloured; used to mark territory.

First aid

In an emergency, veterinary advice should be sought at once. The gerbil should be picked up carefully and taken to the vet in a small secure container lined with hay. Telephone first if necessary to check that the vet will be there.

Falls   Gerbils can usually cope with minor falls in the cage or gerbilarium in the course of play, but a fall when being handled, for example, could be serious. Return the gerbil to its nest and leave it alone to recover while keeping a quiet watch on it. If shock seems to persist or the gerbil moves with difficulty, it should be taken immediately to the vet.

Heat exhaustion   Heat exhaustion is potentially fatal and must be taken seriously. A gerbil with heat exhaustion lies still, trembling slightly. The cage or gerbilarium should be taken to a well-ventilated, darkened room and the gerbils left to recover with no stress of any kind. Make sure that the water bottle is filled with a clean, fresh supply.

Wounds   Fighting is one of the commonest causes of death among gerbils, which can inflict deep wounds on each other with their claws and incisor teeth. Housing them in compatible groups (see pages 6–9) normally avoids this problem.

Minor wounds resulting from fighting or other causes may be bathed with a mild antiseptic. Deeper wounds need veterinary attention because of the risk of infection and possible abscesses if a wound heals over trapping bacteria inside.

Gerbils make good, attentive parents until the young can fend for themselves.

Fits Some gerbils are prone to fits or seizures, most often caused by overhandling, overtiredness or other stress factors. Death occasionally follows, but more often the gerbil will recover if it is left alone. Gerbils prone to fits should not, however, be used for breeding.

Ailments

Gerbils are unlikely to fall victim to disease if they are kept clean, dry and warm, and fed a suitable diet. Most of these ailments are rare, and few gerbil owners will have to cope with them. Observation of basic hygiene such as the disposal of unwanted food and the cleaning schedules mentioned on page 25 will normally prevent the outbreak of any disease.

The time you spend every day observing and playing with your gerbils can be used also for a routine check on the cleanliness of the ears, nose, eyes and anus, and on the condition of the coat.

If any of the ailments listed below is suspected, the affected animal should be isolated as soon as possible. It is as well to have a reserve cage available for this purpose, with a clean food bowl, water bottle and one or two playthings. When the emergency is over, the reserve cage should be thoroughly cleaned and disinfected so that it is ready if needed again.

Albino gerbil

Colds Some gerbils may be subject to colds which have the same symptoms as a cold in humans – a runny nose and eyes accompanied by sneezing and poor breathing. As with humans, the cold normally clears itself up after a couple of days.

As also with humans, however, a cold can spread among gerbils, and the affected animal should be isolated until the symptoms have disappeared. On no account should human cold remedies be administered. If colds do not clear up within two or three days, the vet should be consulted.

Diarrhoea Unpleasantly smelly droppings and staining under the tail are signs that a gerbil has diarrhoea. Early veterinary attention is essential as the loss of fluid through diarrhoea can be life-threatening.

Fleas Although the gerbil has no flea specific to itself it is possible, although rare, for a gerbil to pick up fleas from cats or dogs. Fleas can be a problem in the best-kept home and on the cleanest pets. A vet should be consulted to obtain a suitable insecticide: remember that fleas' eggs drop off the animal into bedding and carpets, so it will be necessary to treat the surroundings as well as the pets themselves. The gerbils' own bedding and nesting material should be replaced.

Mange   Mange is a condition caused by the presence of the mange mite, which causes baldness, scaliness and a rough, dry coat. The condition can be the result of a poorly balanced diet.

A gerbil with suspected mange should be isolated, and the advice of a vet should be sought urgently.

Sore noses and eyes   Owners sometimes report that their gerbils are suffering from sore noses and sore eyes, sometimes with bleeding and ulceration.

This condition is the direct result of gerbils' gnawing and burrowing habits, which often open up small lesions in the skin. This is particularly likely to happen if the gerbils are gnawing wire bars or wire mesh, or burrowing through dusty, unsuitable material.

Small wounds should be bathed with an antiseptic to prevent their becoming infected. They should then be treated with drugs available from the vet.

The long-term cure for this condition is to rehouse the gerbils where there is less chance of such injury occurring. The introduction of interesting toys into the cage or gerbilarium may provide a diversion from undesirable activities.

Tyzzer's disease   Tyzzer's disease is the most serious endemic gerbil disease likely to be encountered. It is a condition of the liver, with symptoms of diarrhoea, lethargy and weakness, loss of appetite and wasting, followed by collapse. Veterinary help should be sought, but the disease is usually fatal.

Tyzzer's disease is most likely to be found where large numbers of gerbils are kept together. The animals may contract it through the use of food and bedding contaminated by mice. It is best avoided by scrupulous attention to hygiene.

Following an outbreak of Tyzzer's disease, it is best to start again with new disease-free stock from a reputable breeder. All old bedding and toys must be destroyed and the cage or gerbilarium thoroughly cleaned and disinfected.

Reproduction

Rapidly developing young in the nest at five days old, now showing fur.

BREEDING GERBILS

A word of warning is necessary for owners who wish to breed gerbils. Once a pair have started mating, they will continue to do so, and this could result in somewhere between a dozen and forty young in a year. Before the gerbils are allowed to breed, owners should ensure that they know of good homes for any young which they do not wish to keep themselves.

REPRODUCTIVE LIFE

The length of the reproductive life varies considerably. Some females finish breeding at the age of seven months, others at twenty months. During their fertile life, the females come into season every six days, approximately, and again immediately after giving birth.

Some gerbils reach the age of puberty, when they are capable of breeding, at eight weeks; others not before twelve weeks.

Since pregnancy lasts about twenty-four days, it seems to follow that a female gerbil living with her mate permanently may give birth to a litter a month.

In fact, breeding is controlled by many factors, and some gerbils have only three or four litters in their lifetime; the average is six or seven and the maximum number of litters that can be expected is about ten.

Newborn litter, shown here life-size. Note the dark red skin colour.

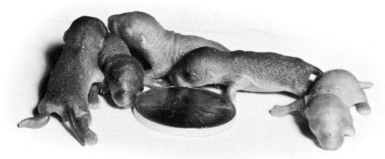

MATING BEHAVIOUR

The female remains on heat for five hours or more each day she is in season and mating seems to be most often observed in the early evening.

The male's mating behaviour is noisy and obvious, with much drumming of the hind feet and chasing around in pursuit of the female. The male follows a repetitive pattern of behaviour, alternately mounting the female, and grooming himself.

Although a female which is housed with a male permanently will accept his advances and live with him companionably it is very difficult indeed to pair up adult gerbils. A female, suddenly presented with a new male, would almost certainly attack him unless they had been introduced with great tact and skill.

PREGNANCY

Pregnancy lasts about twenty-four days, and the female may gain approximately 28g/1oz in weight. She needs to be handled only gently, and given a high protein diet and she may take more water than usual.

NESTING BOX

Both the sexes are good parents, and will share the task of shredding kitchen paper to make a nest for the young, positioning it according to temperature and light. Since these are by nature fossorial, or underground animals, it should be possible for those housed in a cage to rear their litter in the dark, as they would in the wild.

Nesting box

The provision of a wooden nesting box makes this possible. The nesting box not only provides privacy and darkness for the young and for a nervous mother, but keeps the family together for warmth and suckling.

BIRTH

When she gives birth, the female will herself eat the placentas, or afterbirths, and care for her family with no help from the owner. The presence of the male does not upset her, although unwanted human interference may do so, so resist the temptation to check up on the newborn gerbils.

The young may be suckled for as long as twenty-eight days. If the female becomes pregnant again immediately after giving birth, as is possible, the first litter would need to be removed from her on the twenty-second day, to allow her respite to prepare for another litter two days later.

The young

The young are born very underdeveloped, being blind and hairless with a dark red skin colour. Faint crying noises from the nest will betray the presence of perhaps six babies, but they should not be disturbed for several days. There is always a risk that the young will be eaten by the mother if she, or they, are unduly disturbed while they are very young.

It is best for the young to be left with the parents for the first four weeks of life. Both the adults will care for them, keeping them warm and bundling them back into the nesting box as their legs strengthen and they begin to explore outside.

If the female is ready to give birth to another litter on the twenty-fourth day, the first litter will need to be removed from her on the twenty-second day. At this age they will need a temperature of 20°–24°C/68°–75°F, although those not weaned until the fourth week will be able to withstand lower temperatures of 15°–21°C/60°–70°F.

The young can be housed together in a colony up to the age of six to eight weeks. They must be given nesting boxes and shredded bedding, and fed on small seeds, canary rearing food and a little washed fresh fruit or vegetables.

In the early weeks young gerbils will live together happily, indulging in much play and mock fighting. After six to eight weeks the play turns to real fighting, and at this stage the young must be separated into their adult groups (see pages 6–7). These must be decided on by the age of ten weeks, when the young males are capable of mating. New homes must be found for all young gerbils you do not wish to keep.

For the pet keeper who does not want the great worry of disposing of surplus litters, a pair of females would be more suitable than a breeding pair. Two females will be excellent companions for each other and a constant source of fascination to their owner. It is not without reason that gerbils have become such firm favourites in such a short time.

Note, however, that male gerbils must not be housed together or they will fight.

The happy family atmosphere of a young gerbil family persists until the young are six to eight weeks old. Then it gives way to competition for space, which leads to fighting. At this stage, the young must be separated.

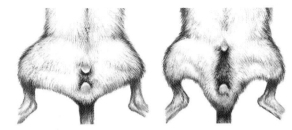

Sexing gerbils
Left Female gerbil showing much shorter urino-genital distance.

Right Long urino-genital distance denotes male gerbil.

Your questions answered

I have been told that gerbils are easy to handle, but mine struggle and try to jump out of my hands, and sometimes bite me. What can I do to train them?
A gerbil is easily alarmed by sudden, jerky movements. Always approach it from the front, talking quietly to it at the same time. Stroke its heads and ears until it feels confident in your presence. Then, still moving slowly and deliberately, cup it into your hands and hold it firmly but lightly. If it still struggles, return it to its cage or gerbilarium and try again another day. It will soon learn that no harm can come to it from being handled by its owner. Gerbil bites are harmless, but it is wise to treat the bite with a little disinfectant or antiseptic cream.

Do I need to brush my gerbils' coats?
No. Gerbils living together will groom each other, and this grooming is an important part of their social lives. Provided you feed your gerbils a properly balanced diet, their coats will normally remain in good, clean condition.

My gerbils' claws seem very long. Is this natural, or should I do something about it?
In the wild, gerbils' claws are digging tools and wear down naturally. In captivity, especially in a cage, this may not happen, so your gerbils' claws may become overlong. Trimming the claws without damaging the sensitive core is difficult, and you should ask your vet to do this.

Is it all right to leave gerbils to look after themselves for the weekend?
It is far better to arrange for a friend or neighbour to come in and give them fresh food and water, or to take them to the friend's house. As gerbils neither hoard food nor gorge themselves, it *is* possible to leave them for a day or so with a good supply of food and a full water bottle, but do arrange to have someone to check them every day in case of an accident or a power cut.

My gerbils sometimes show the symptoms of heat exhaustion, lying still and hardly breathing, even when the temperature is not high. What is the explanation?

There are two possible reasons for this behaviour. One is that the gerbils suffer from fits. They normally recover if left alone, but they should not be used for breeding as they may pass the tendency on to the next generation. An alternative possibility is that the gerbils are 'playing dead' to deceive an enemy. This is an instinct that has been observed among gerbils in the wild if they are frightened. Your gerbils may have been alarmed by a sudden noise, or by the presence of a cat or dog in the room (or even, in the case of a cat, outside the window). Always ensure that, however securely your gerbils are housed, other domestic pets do not have access to the room where they live.

My gerbils' teeth seem to be very prominent, and can be seen when their mouths are closed. Should anything be done about this?

You are not providing your gerbils with enough materials which they can gnaw to keep their teeth trimmed. The teeth should not be visible when a gerbil's mouth is closed. Buy a gnawing block from a pet shop or put one or two pieces of untreated wood, the harder the better, in the cage. The eventual result of overgrown teeth, if no action is taken, will be that your gerbils will be unable to feed.

Can my gerbils catch a cold from me?

Yes. If you have a cold or influenza you should avoid handling them or preparing their food. Ask someone else in the family to look after them until you are better.

Is the Mongolian gerbil the only species of the gerbil family, or are there others which can be kept as pets?

The gerbil family contains over eighty different species, ranging from the tiny Egyptian gerbil, which is only about 12cm/5in from head to tail compared with the Mongolian gerbil's 20cm/8in, to the Indian gerbil with a length of 45cm/18in. The little Egyptian gerbils are sometimes kept as pets in the home, and the large Libyan gerbils, 40cm/16in in length, can be kept in heated outside sheds. But the Mongolian gerbil has been shown to be the easiest to keep in Britain because of its adaptability to domestic conditions and also for its free availability from pet shops and breeders.

Life history

Scientific name	*Meriones unguiculatus*
Gestation period	24 days (approx.)
Litter size	4–6 (average)
Birth weight	2·5–3·5g
Eyes open	16–20 days
Weaning age	21–28 days
Weaning weight	11–18g
Puberty	65–85 days
Adult weight	males: 117g/4oz (average) females: 100g/3½oz (average)
Best age to breed	males: 140+ days females: 100+ days
Retire from breeding	males: 22 months females: 18 months
Oestrus (or season)	Every six days throughout the year
Duration of oestrus	5+ hours
Life expectancy	2–3 years

Record card

Record sheet for your own gerbils

<table>
<tr>
<td>

(photograph or portrait)

</td>
<td>

(photograph or portrait)

</td>
</tr>
</table>

Name ACE

Date of birth
(actual or estimated)

Variety   Sex Male

Colour/Description gray/silver

Smallest

Feeding notes

Name

Date of birth
(actual or estimated)

Variety   Sex

Colour/Description

Medical notes

Veterinary surgeon's name

Practice address

Surgery hours

Tel. no.

Index